This Book Has Been
Presented to
Leavenworth Library
In Honor of
Eliza Powers
By
Mr. and Mrs. Don Ritchey
Family Day 2000

Breathtaking
NOSES

HANA MACHOTKA

Morrow Junior Books
New York

for Thor and Phaedra

The text type is 20 point Eras Book.
Jacket design by Karen Palinko.

Printed in Singapore at Tien Wah Press.

1 2 3 4 5 6 7 8 9 10

Library of Congress Cataloging-in-Publication Data
Machotka, Hana.
   Breathtaking noses / Hana Machotka.
      p.   cm.
   Summary: Examines the noses of a variety of
different animals and describes how they function.
   ISBN 0-688-09526-7.—0-688-09527-5 (lib. bdg.)
   1. Nose—Juvenile literature.   [1. Nose. 2. Animals.]
I. Title.
QM505.M33   1992
596'.01826—dc20   91-12252   CIP   AC

Acknowledgments

My photographs were taken at Muscoot Farms, Somers, N.Y.; the Catskill Game Farm, Palenville, N.Y.; Bronx Zoo, N.Y.; the Greenberg Nature Center, Greenberg, N.Y.; The New York Aquarium, Brooklyn; and the Orange County Fair, Middletown, N.Y.

Special thanks go to Bruce Lawder and Karen Stern of the Greenberg Nature Center for giving so generously of their time and efforts; Dr. Francis Fay of the University of Alaska for sharing his expertise on walrus; Ann Hollaran of The New York Aquarium for answering my questions about their walrus; Brigitte Mirow for helping me with her dog; Dr. Allison V. Andors of the American Museum of Natural History in New York for assistance on researching swans; and Shannon Woodcock and Chico of the Woodcock Elephants for their persistence in helping me get my photos.

As ever, thanks to my editor, Andrea Curley, and to art director Barbara Fitzsimmons and designer Karen Palinko for their support and contributions.

A nose is the outermost part of an animal's face, located between the eyes. The nose includes nostrils and is usually involved in smelling, breathing, and producing sounds. Some noses also have special jobs to do, and sometimes they have very unusual shapes with which to do them.

The king of noses is surely the elephant's long, muscular trunk. It is powerful enough to uproot a tree, yet delicate enough to pick up a straw with a sensitive "finger" at its end. The elephant's sense of smell is so acute that its nose can detect a person several miles away. Can you think of some other possible uses for this unusual nose? As you look at the noses in this book, see if you can figure out how each one helps the animal live in its world.

SWAN

These nostrils are used for breathing.
Scientists suspect that swans also have
a good sense of smell. This may help them
find food, identify other swans, and locate
their nests.

When swans duck their heads underwater,
a flap seals the nose so that water and debris
cannot get into it. Then the swan uses a sharp
"nail" at the tip of its bill to pull up edible
plants. Swans can drink fresh or salt water.
They have a special gland over each eye that
removes salt from salt water. The salt drips out
through the nose and is tossed away with a
shake of the head.

A nose that's also a powerful digging tool belongs to a…

PIG

The pig's excellent sense of smell helps it identify other pigs. It also helps the pig find mushrooms, insects, worms, and slugs, even those that are several feet underground. Then this hard, flat nose will act like a shovel to root out the tasty morsels from the dirt. It is also handy for opening a barnyard gate.

The pig's very special nose helps it make a variety of sounds. A male pig has a special "song" that attracts a female. A piglet gives off repeated grunts and shrieks if it becomes lost. When the baby is found, the other pigs will touch noses with it in greeting.

One of the most sensitive noses of all belongs to a...

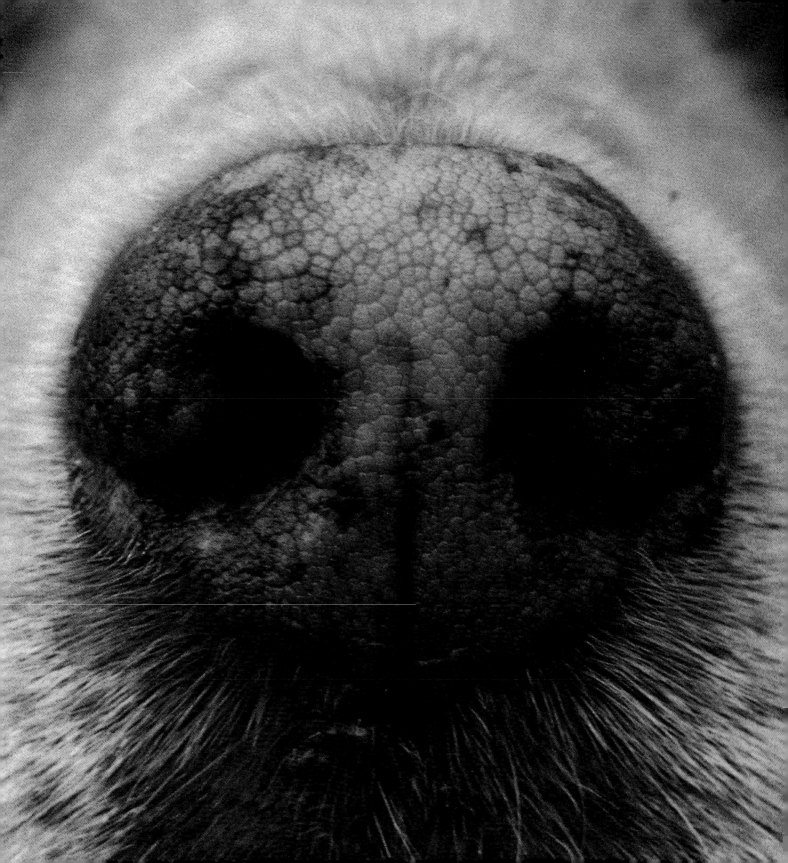

DOG

Dogs are constantly smelling everything around them. Odors give a dog an enormous amount of information about its environment. A dog's large nose contains a very big smelling organ that is perhaps a million times more sensitive to smell than is our own.

The dog uses its sense of smell to recognize members of its pack and to identify intruders. With the help of its nose, a dog can follow a person or animal over long distances, even if the trail is old or covered. A dog's nose can tell not only how old a scent is but in which direction it leads!

The long, slitlike nostrils on this nose belong to a…

CAMEL

The muscles around these nostrils will close up the camel's nose to protect it from blowing sand and dust—*or* ice and snow (some camels live in cold climates). If debris does get into the nostrils, hairs in the camel's nose will help filter it out. The soft lining of the camel's nose can wet, warm, or cool incoming air, helping the animal to live in many different kinds of environments.

The camel's upper lip is split, or *cleft*. This shape allows moisture to collect from the camel's breath, helping to save water. A camel can go without drinking for about two weeks. With its excellent sense of smell, the camel can find water far away.

A soft nose with nostrils that can seal up tight underwater belongs to a…

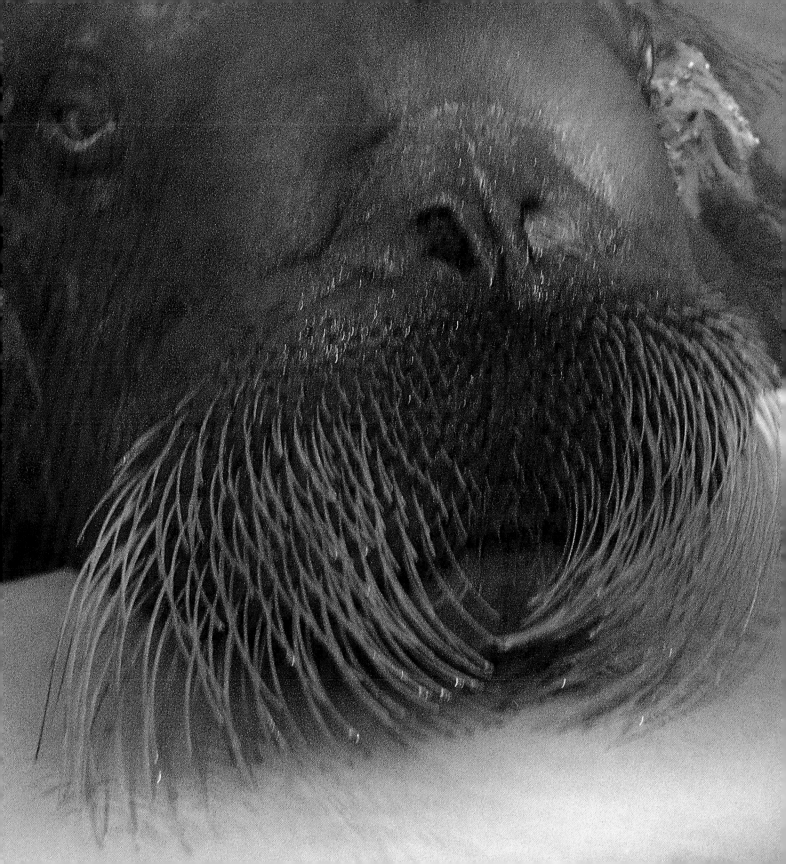

WALRUS

When a walrus dives underwater to feed on mussels and clams, it closes its nostrils completely to keep water out. It can hold its breath for over ten minutes while it feels for food with its whiskers in the bottom mud. Its powerful nose roots in the soft mud, while the movable bristles help loosen the shellfish and direct them into the walrus's mouth.

Once out of the water, the walrus opens its nostrils to breathe. Back on land, a walrus's good sense of smell helps a mother find her baby in a large herd.

We have seen how different noses help various animals survive in the world. Have you thought of some other ways in which an elephant's trunk can be useful? It can guide a baby elephant, hold another elephant's tail, pick tasty leaves off a tall tree, siphon water for a drink or shower, and trumpet a call to another elephant.

Do you think the elephant's trunk would serve a camel as well? Why might the pig's "digging" nose be hard while the walrus's nose is soft?

When you have a chance, watch how different animals use their noses. Noses are important tools for finding out about the world. But look out—those animals may use their noses to find out about you!